SCENES AROUND THE SOUT

John C Morgan

© John C Morgan and Noodle Books 2014

ISBN 978-1-909328-23-5

First published in 2014 by Kevin Robertson
under the **NOODLE BOOKS** imprint
PO Box 279
Corhampton
SOUTHAMPTON
SO32 3ZX

www.noodlebooks.co.uk

Printed in England by Berforts Information Press

Front Cover: 6PUL 3006 forms the 14.00 Ore to Victoria as it joins the Brighton line at Keymer Junction on 11th August 1963.

Title page: Ugly Duckling (a matter of personal choice!), Q1 class 33027 heads a southbound freight through Romsey on 5th August 1964.

This page: The "early symbol" as designated in the model railway world – the lion and wheel emblem on the side of a 2BIL emu, 28th June 1967.

Opposite: On a bright 17th February 1962, West Country 34092 *City of Wells* runs into Salisbury from the west.

Rear cover: Salisbury to Southampton via Redbridge is the route of West Country no. 34092 *City of Wells* passing Romsey on 5th August 1964.

SCENES AROUND THE SOUTHERN.

Introduction.

To begin, I would start by thanking Kevin Robertson for the idea to produce this book from my own 35mm colour slides of the Southern. While showing him some specific slides for possible inclusion in "Southern Way", he suggested that the collection could be published as a separate volume. All the views were taken in the 1960s and early 70s , and cover the "green" period, with just one or two exceptions straying into the "blue". Technically, they were all taken on an Agfa *Super Silette* camera with Prontor SVS shutter, using Agfa CT18 film at 100 ASA. Lighting was assessed with a Sixtry lightmeter. My policy was always to use the fastest shutter speed whenever possible, this being 1/500 sec., except when it was obviously too dark.

Back in 1994 I produced a colour book specifically on Southern Electrics, now long out of print, entitled "Southern EMUs in Colour". This was published by Ian Allan, and with their permission, a few of those pictures are included in the present work.

Until I was married in 1963 I lived in Cheam, and commuted daily to Euston where I was employed in the Chief Civil Engineer's office of the London Midland Region. After getting married, we moved to Burgess Hill, which accounts for the higher number of pictures taken on the Brighton line. Not surprisingly I have a certain affection for the Brighton Line (I commuted on it for some 32 years!), even so I considered that the end of April 1972 was the cut-off point (also the end of the 'Belle').

The book is divided into rough sections but deliberately nor regimented, plus a few singleton views and pages. There are also two pieces allocated particularly to the Brighton Belle, and the Bournemouth Belle and I have included the timings I made on these two trains. There is also a similar record of a trip on the Somerset & Dorset from Bournemouth West through to Bath Green Park.

John C Morgan

Redhill.

Left: Standing in Platform 1b at Redhill in the late afternoon of 26th September 1964, is 'U' class no. 31639. Of note is the plate to prevent the coupling swinging backwards.

Above: This appears to be on the scrap siding of Redhill MPD – Maunsell 'Q' class 0-6-0 no. 30531 awaits its fate also on 26th September 1964.

Opposite: Class 73 no. E6013 in the new livery of blue/grey stands in the Up side sidings at Redhill on the morning of 10th July 1967, significantly on the day after steam was retired from the Southern Region. (A comparative view of an example from the earlier series of ED is on p47.)

Top left: Your author was up at the crack of dawn (remembering he started out from Burgess Hill) on 14th May 1965 when 2-6-0 'N' class no. 31811 hauled a southbound freight through Redhill – the clock on the tower reads 07.10!

Top right: A few weeks earlier than the 'Q' class shown on the previous page, 'N' class 2-6-0 no. 31827 waits in the scrap siding at Redhill MPD on 18th July 1964.

Left: An unusual visitor to Redhill on 18th July 1964 was WR Hymek diesel hydraulic (subsequently Class 35) no. D7059 waiting in Platform 2. The engine would likely have arrived on a working from Reading.

Burgess Hill.

Top: Not very many of the 4LAVs acquired the full frontal yellow end before their demise, but 2931 was one unit that did. It is standing in Burgess Hill Down platform forming a stopping train from Victoria to Brighton on 29th August 1967.

Bottom right : Half a mile or so south of Burgess Hill, there is a public footpath that runs alongside the Down line. On 4th February 1967, the foliage had not grown up enough to obscure 4LAV 2933 on a London Bridge to Brighton stopping service.

Inset above: On 29th May 1965, the station at Christs Hospital had not been transformed into a bus shelter – what a pity such interesting architecture has to be removed just because we cannot afford to pay for its upkeep!

This 4LAV, no. 2942, is seen before the days of small yellow ends, on 7th March 1964, forming a Victoria to Brighton stopping service at Burgess Hill. The down platform shows signs of having been recently extended.

Another 4LAV, this time a recently repainted set 2949 approaches Burgess Hill on 23rd July 1966. The train was seen from Station Road overbridge – nicely maintained cutting slopes, which would not be recognisable today in the vast amount of undergrowth.

Basingstoke.
Merchant Navy 35003 *Royal Mail* heads the Up Atlantic Coast Express (non-stop from Salisbury to Waterloo) complete with headboard through Basingstoke on 29th September 1962. On the left is a gantry of LSWR lower quadrant pneumatic signals.

'U' Class 2-6-0 no. 31804 waits to turn left for Reading from Platform 4 at Basingstoke (the Up Slow) on 29th September 1962. Out of sight to the left are the platforms of the former Great Western station at Basingstoke. The engine will be seen to be AWS fitted - hence the battery box on the framing.

Left: B R Standard 5MT no. 73112 approaches Basingstoke on the Down Slow with a stopping train to Salisbury, 29th September 1962.
Bottom: No 30837, an S15 based on the original LSWR 4-6-0 design although built by the Southern Railway in the late 20s. The train is approaching Basingstoke on an Up freight, again on 29th September 1962. Note the six-wheeled tender attached. The containers may well contain meat imported through Southampton Docks.

Left: While travelling to Basingstoke on the Down Slow on 27th July 1963, we were overtaken by BR Standard Class 5MT 73115 with a Southampton Docks boat train. The location is near to the Sturt Lane Junction aqueduct.

Bottom: Another Maunsell 'S15' and from its external condition somewhat travel weary, seen here with an eight-wheeled tender. This is another Up freight running through the Up Slow, platform 4, at Basingstoke on 5th August 1964.

On 12th October 1963, my wife and I had a day trip from Burgess Hill via Brighton, Portsmouth & Southsea, Southampton, and Bournemouth intending to travel on the Somerset & Dorset to Bath Green Park. We caught the 07.08 from Burgess Hill, giving us 24 minutes to transfer to the 07.47 from Brighton. At Portsmouth & Southsea we had 18 minutes before the 09.30 departure for Southampton. None of these journeys I had bothered to time, but the next train was steam hauled – 34010 with 7 coaches on to Bournemouth Central. This was the 10.30 which departed 7 mins late but had picked up 3 mins by Brockenhurst. We lost a further 2 mins at the station, but then with an 87mph burst down Hinton Admiral bank, we arrived in Bournemouth Central just 2 mins late at 11.16. For the short hop round to Bournemouth West we were reduced to 4 coaches, and hauled backwards by 34045. A full record of

Saturday 12th October 1963.			75007 and 4 coaches.		
Station	Miles	d	Due	Actual	Speed
Bournemouth West	71	d	11.40	00 00	1L
Bournemouth West Junc	70½			02 43	34
Branksome	69¾			03 24	40
Parkstone	68½			05 07	51½/57½
Poole	66¾	a	08	07 41	-
		d	11.49	00 00	1L
Holes Bay Junc	66				35/50
Creekmore Halt	64½			03 40	47
Broadstone	63¼	a	08	05 51	-
		d	11.58	00 00	2E
Corfe Mullen Halt	61½				53
Corfe Mullen Junc	60¼			05 14	59½
Bailey Gate	58½			06 59	62½
Spetisbury Halt	55½			09 52	59/64½
Charlton Marshall Halt	54			11 30	52
Blandford Forum	52¼	a	16	14 29	-
		d	12.15	00 00	5L
Stourpaine & Durweston Halt	49½			04 37	54½
Shillingstone	46¾			08 23	sigs
				16 17	stop
					50
Sturminster Newton	43¾	a	16	21 26	-
		d	12.32	00 00	10L
Milepost 41	41			04 13	54½
Stalbridge	39¾	a	06	05 51	-
		d	12.39	00 00	9½L
Henstridge	38¼			02 50	47
Templecombe Lower	36½			05 50	sigs
				07 30	stop
					56
Wincanton	33			12 47	22 pws
Milepost 31	31			16 01	53
Cole	28¾			18 35	51
Evercreech Junction	26	a	23	22 06	-

Saturday 12th October 1963.			75007 and 4 coaches.		
Station	Miles	d	Due	Actual	Speed
Evercreech Junction	26	a	23	22 06	-
		d	13.03	00 00	8½L
Evercreech New	24½			03 31	32½
Milepost 23	23			06 57	21½
Milepost 22½	22½			08 22	20
Milepost 22	22			09 55	19½
Shepton Mallet	21¼			11 19	42½
Winsor Hill Tunnel S Portal	19¾			13 44	29
Milepost 19	19			15 32	26
Masbury Halt	18¼			17 52	23½
Summit (811 ft.)	17¾			19 16	18½
Binegar	16½			20 57	51
Moorewood Signalbox	15¼			22 35	55
Chilcompton & Downside	14			23 56	55½
Chilcompton Tunnel	13¼			24 51	50½
Midsomer Norton & Welton	12			26 24	45
Radstock North	10¼			29 05	34
Shoscombe & Single Hill Halt	8			33 05	46
Wellow	6¼			34 29	44
Midford	3¾			38 45	35½
Coombe Down Tunnel N Portal	2			41 50	34
Devonshire Tunnel N Portal	1¼			42 53	44
Bath Junction Signalbox	0			45 15	22½
Bath Green Park	0½	a	50	47 20	-

our run from there on to Bath is shown in the table above. En route, as we waited in Blandford Forum for the single line to clear, I recorded BR Standard 5MT 73164 coming south. The return journey was also interesting. I had decided on a different route home – the 17.23 from Bath Spa via Westbury, Salisbury, and Southampton to Fratton. D7043 with 1 x CCT and 7 coaches took us to Westbury where we shed 3 coaches. At Salisbury we exchanged D7043 for 76009, and ran to Fratton where we arrived at 20.17. However, due to a derailment at Portcreek Junction, we caught the 20.14 to Brighton which was delayed for half an hour. The Brighton arrival was just in time to see the 21.58 departing without us on it! Enjoyable, but a long day!

Above: Ivatt 2MT 2-6-2T no. 41254 approaches Bournemouth Central from the Branksome direction on 22nd May 1965. The line on the right is the continuation of the carriage siding.

Right: 'The Way Forward' – from the cab of a very grimy West Country no. 34041 *Wilton* at Waterloo, 22nd May 1965. Unfortunately, I had to travel on the train!

Clapham Junction.

Right: BR Standard 2-6-2T class 3MT 82024 appears to be in a rather run down condition just north of Clapham Junction on 30th July 1964. The process to resurrect one of these locomotives has already begun at Sheffield Park on the Bluebell Railway.

Bottom: Ivatt 2-6-2T class 2MT no. 41312 takes a break during shunting duties at Clapham (Junction) Yard, 3rd June 1967. 41312 now resides on the Mid Hants Railway.

Left: Was it an ECS working to Southampton Docks that had necessitated just a three coach train? Class 5MT 73029 seen approaching Clapham Junction on 30th October 1964.

Bottom: Running light between Clapham Junction and West London Junction on 3rd June 1967 is West Country 34023 *"Blackmore Vale"*, bereft of nameplate and before it moved to Longmoor and then the Bluebell Railway for preservation.

Prior to its journey down the South Western main line to its final work place on the Isle of Wight, ex-London Transport unit no. 4VEC 043 rests near West London Junction. The first electric (former LT tube) tube trains used on the Island were divided into two types , the 4VEC and the 3TIS ('Vectis' being the Roman name for the Isle of Wight). (The sets had first been hauled to storage at Micheldever before being fitted out at Eastleigh and Wimbledon. They then ran trials on the South Western main line before being shipped from Portsmouth to Ryde.)

Lord Nelson class no. 30862 *Lord Collingwood* on a Down Bournemouth train approaches Clapham Junction on 21st July 1962. The engine was withdrawn from service not long afterwards with one of the nameplates presented to Stephen Collingwood Townroe, the retiring District Motive Power Superintendent from Eastleigh.

Above: En route from Nine Elms to Waterloo is Lord Nelson no. 30862 *Lord Collingwood* on 21st July 1962.

Left: Q1 class 0-6-0 no. 33006 rests inside Guildford MPD on 4th June 1965. The Q1s had been associated with Guildford almost from their introduction in 1942. 1965 would also be the last time they were to be seen in the area.

Top: M7 class 0-4-4T no. 30249 on an ECS working about to depart from Waterloo on 29th September 1962. Usually empty stock was drawn back to Clapham for servicing but in busy times locations further out would be used. The Palace of Westminster's Victoria Tower is in the background.

Bottom: Ex-GWR pannier tank no. 9670 on an Up ECS working to Waterloo approaching Vauxhall on 29th September 1962. Several members of the class were used for a while on such duties being based at Nine Elms.

Opposite: A limited number of Brush Type 4 locomotives (later class 47) were allocated to the Southern Region in 1966/67 mainly to cover deficiencies in the declining steam fleet. Even so they were only used into Waterloo on occasional workings, and from 1 January 1967 on the 'Bournemouth Belle'. Here we have an exception, D1926 working the 15.30 Waterloo to Bournemouth, seen approaching Vauxhall on 30th May 1967. The headcode '92' was used by non-steam workings to indicate a semi-fast service to Bournemouth. ('91' was the fast, and '93' the stopping service.)

Vauxhall and Wimbledon.

Left: Battle of Britain no. 34059 *Sir Archibald Sinclair* (now on the Bluebell Railway) approaches Vauxhall with the 18.00 Waterloo to Basingstoke, 21st April 1965.

Above: Merchant Navy no. 35007 *Aberdeen Commonwealth* runs light to Waterloo, 21st April 1965.

Opposite top left: Everything is happening at once at Vauxhall on 21st April 1965, as BR Standard 5MT no. 73114 heads the 18.09 Waterloo to Basingstoke.

Opposite top right: Converted West Country no. 34013 *Okehampton* passes Wimbledon 'C' Signalbox (on the Down side) possibly with an Up race special (?), 3rd June 1967. The white painted buffers and smokebox hinges were a feature of several steam engines towards the very end.

Bottom left: Merchant Navy no. 35015 *Rotterdam Lloyd* in full cry with the down Atlantic Coast Express, seen passing Wimbledon 'A' signalbox, 3rd June 1962. Bottom right: Converted West Country 34004 *Yeovil* on a shorter train, the 10.55 from Waterloo, approaches Wimbledon on 3rd March 1962.

On 7th November 1964, Battle of Britain no. 34057 *Biggin Hill* is just starting the climb from Exeter St Davids to Exeter Central with the "Meldon Ballast". At the rear the working is being banked by two Pannier tanks, 4666 + 4694.

Standing in the Yard at Exmouth Junction MPD are BR Standards 4MT 80039 and 3MT 82039 on 7th November 1964 - the latter engine in green livery. The red mark from the nameplate position of the unidentified 'Merchant Navy' in the background is not explained.

The Bournemouth Belle.

The first Merchant Navy Pacific to be built, no. 35001 *Channel Packet,* originally numbered 21C1, races through Wimbledon with the Down Bournemouth Belle, 25th May 1963. The last day of steam working on the Belle was scheduled for Saturday 31st December 1966, when West Country 34093 *Saunton* took 2 BGs and 9 Pullmans from Waterloo on the 12.30 to Bournemouth. The timings were diagrammed for a Merchant Navy locomotive, but we had to suffice with the West Country. Full details are shown on the spreadsheet opposite. It took some time to recover from the climb to Steventon, but we then raced to 89 mph through Shawford before signals around Swaythling/St Denys curtailed a very fast run to Southampton, even so still arriving 4 mins early. A 2 mins late restart became 12 mins late into Bournemouth after many unfortunate signal checks from New Milton onwards.

Saturday 31st December 1966.   34093 + 2 BGs + 9 Pullmans

The Bournemouth Belle.   419 tons tare, 440 tons gross.

Train: BG S81153, Car 36, Car 76, Loraine, Lucille, Phyllis, Ursula, Car 64, Car 303, Car 34, BG S81050

Station	M.Ch.	d	Due	Actual	Speed
Waterloo	00-00	d	12.30	00 00	Time
Vauxhall	01-26			03 58	34½
Queens Road Battersea	02-55			05 51	45½
Clapham Junction	03-71			07 33	42
Earlsfield	05-48			09 46	50½
Wimbledon	07-17			11 45	52
Raynes Park	08-55			13 20	54½
New Malden	09-64			14 28	57½
Berrylands	10-75			15 37	62½
Surbiton	12-02			16 42	62
Hampton Court Junc	13-26			17 55	63
Esher	14-31			18 53	67
Hersham	15-74			20 18	68
Walton-on-Thames	17-06			21 18	65½
Weybridge	19-09			23 09	65
Byfleet & New Haw	20-31			24 23	67
West Byfleet	21-53			25 34	64½
Woking	24-26			28 07	61½
Woking Junc	24-61			28 35	61
Brookwood	27-79			31 44	60/59
Sturt Lane Junc	32-16			35 57	62½
Farnborough	33-18			36 52	62
Bramshot Halt	35-50			39 08	63½
Fleet	36-39			39 56	65½
Winchfield	39-67			42 51	64½
Hook	42-14			45 00	63½
Newnham Siding	43-55			46 22	62½
Barton Mill Signalbox	46-75			49 22	63
Basingstoke	47-63			50 11	61
Worting Junc Signalbox	50-20			52 59	51½
Wootton Signalbox	52-39			55 48	45
Steventon Signalbox	53-75			57 32	47½
Litchfield Tunnel	55-65			59 48	46½
Micheldever	58-06			62 33	48½
Weston Signalbox	60-15			64 59	54½
Wallers Ash Tunnel S Portal	62-44			67 17	70½
Winchester Junc	64-46			68 42	80
Winchester City	66-37			70 17	84
St Cross Signalbox	67-60			71 13	84
Shawford	69-50			72 30	89
Eastleigh	73-22			75 16	84
Southampton Airport	74-68			76 22	80
Swaythling	75-54			77 07	34½ sigs
St Denys	77-08			79 05	45/11 sigs
Northam Junc Signalbox	78-16			81 57	21
sigs				84 19	2'26" stop
Southampton Central	79-19	a	93	89 08	-
		d	14.04	00 00	2L
Millbrook	80-15			02 54	38½
Redbridge	81-70			05 09	52
Totton	82-40			05 50	54
Lyndhurst Road	85-32			08 44	56
Beaulieu Road	88-06			11 30	60
Woodfidley Gates	89-59			13 12	64/73
Brockenhurst	92-65			15 36	64½
Lymington Junc	93-60			16 31	62
Sway	95-45			19 28	14½ pws
New Milton	98-44			24 49	55/15 sigs
Hinton Admiral	101-05			29 41	stop 38"
Christchurch	104-28			38 05	stop 36"
Pokesdown	106-24			42 48	27
Boscombe	106-67			44 02	29½
sigs	107-40				3'00" stop
Bournemouth Central	108-02	a	41	51 33	-

29

Saturday 31st December 1966. 34047+ 2 BGs + 9 Pullmans

The Bournemouth Belle. 419 tons tare, 435 tons gross

Train: BG S81050, Car 34, Car 303, Car 64, Ursula, Phyllis,
Lucille, Loraine, Car 76, Car 36, BG S81153

Station	M.Ch.	d	Due	Actual	Speed
Bournemouth Central	108-02	d	16.37	00 00	Time
Boscombe	106-67			03 17	39
Pokesdown	106-24			04 06	51
Christchurch	104-28			06 02	68
Hinton Admiral	101-05			09 06	59½
New Milton	98-44			11 31	61½
Sway	95-45			14 08	72
Lymington Junc	93-60			15 46	67
Brockenhurst	92-65			16 38	68½
Woodfidley Gates	89-59			19 13	71
Beaulieu Road	88-06			20 36	72/74
Lyndhurst Road	85-32			22 53	66/73
Totton	82-40			25 38	48
Redbridge	81-70			26 20	50½/55½
Millbrook	80-15			28 25	39½/19½
Southampton Central	79-19	a	36	31 16	-
		d	17.15	00 00	1L
Northam Junc Signalbox	78-16			03 35	23½
St Denys	77-08			05 22	43
Swaythling	75-54			07 09	51½
Southampton Airport	74-68			08 10	59/19 sigs
Eastleigh	73-32			10 37	33½
Shawford	69-50			15 32	56
Shawford Junc Signalbox	68-68			16 23	58
St Cross Signalbox	67-60			17 29	60½
Winchester City	66-37			18 47	61½
Winchester Junc	64-46			20 52	64½
Wallers Ash Tunnel S Portal	62-44			22 23	65
Weston Signalbox	60-15			24 47	64
Micheldever	58-06			26 52	61½
Litchfield Tunnel	55-65			29 16	50
Steventon Signalbox	53-75			31 34	47
Wootton Signalbox	52-39			33 38	37/25
Worting Junc Signalbox	50-20			37 25	48
Basingstoke	47-63			39 49	71
Barton Mill Signalbox	46-75			40 30	74
Newnham Siding	43-55			43 11	77
Hook	42-14			44 18	80
Winchfield	39-67			46 14	79
Fleet	36-39			48 52	81
Bramshot Halt	35-50			49 31	80
Farnborough	33-18			51 33	74½
Sturt Lane Junc	32-16			52 25	79
Brookwood	27-79			56 26	54
Woking Junc	24-61			61 18	21½
Woking	24-26			62 51	15 sigs
West Byfleet	21-53			67 39	55
Byfleet & New Haw	20-31			68 49	66/15½ sigs
Weybridge	19-09			71 50	25½
Walton-on-Thames	17-06			74 38	57
Hersham	15-74			75 43	66
Esher	14-31			77 08	67½
Hampton Court Junc	13-26			78 06	66½
Surbiton	12-02			79 18	66
Berrylands	10-75			80 20	61½
New Malden	09-64			81 37	44
Raynes Park	08-55			83 50	24/20½ pws
Wimbledon	07-17			86 55	39
Earlsfield	05-48			89 11	50
Clapham Junction	03-71			91 30	42
Queens Road Battersea	02-55			93 07	48
Vauxhall	01-26			95 08	25½
Waterloo	00-00	a	98	99 07	-

Having arrived and then had its coaches drawn off, Merchant Navy no. 35003 *Royal Mail* waits to return from Waterloo to Nine Elms MPD for servicing on 17th February 1962.

Waiting by the famous signal gantry at Southampton Central is Merchant Navy no. 35030 *Elder Dempster Lines but* minus its nameplates on 30th May 1967. Less than seven weeks later this engine would haul the very last scheduled steam train into Waterloo before full electrification of the Bournemouth main line.

Salisbury.

A rear end view at the London end of Salisbury station. BR Standard 5MT no. 73043 appears to be backing down to the platform on 7th November 1964. Sitting in the platform on the right is the DEMU service to either Southampton or Portsmouth. The electrification warning flashes on the tender were a feature of all locomotives from the late 1950s, even if as on the Southern there were few locations where overhead wires existed.

Above: Converted Battle of Britain no. 34059 *Sir Archibald Sinclair* starts away from the Down Main Platform 4 at Salisbury on 17th February 1962. The Bulleid design coaches behind will be noted.

Right: Converted West Country no. 34027 *Taw Valley* sits in Platform 4 at Salisbury on 17th February 1962. These days, *Taw Valley* is based on the Severn Valley Railway.

Eastleigh.

A Works visit on 5th August 1964 brought a close-up view of the Raworth/Bullied Co-Co electric locomotive no. 20002. One of the main uses of these locomotives was on the Victoria to Newhaven boat trains but they were also used on freight to Chichester.

Top left: Undergoing some refurbishment in the Works is A1X no. 32662 although looking in rather a sorry state. Originally numbered 62, she was named *Martello*, having been built in 1875.

Top right: An old LSWR design B4 class 0-4-0T was in the early stages of preservation and a return to original condition with cut away cab. Seen here as BR no. 30102, the engine was originally named *Granville*.

Left: D2985 was out in the Yard, these locomotives had succeeded the USA tanks in Southampton Docks and which in turn had succeeded the B4s.

.

Attracting an admiring audience on what was then Platform 3, rebuilt West Country no. 34040 *Crewkerne* brings an inter-regional train through Eastleigh on the Down Fast on 5th August 1964. There were a number of through workings using maroon stock from the SR northwards, this included the Pines Express which had been rerouted via Basingstoke and Reading after 1962.

Top left: Q1 class 0-6-0 no. 33020 was in the Yard. At this stage in the life of steam, having the coupling rods removed was a sure sign the engine was withdrawn. Top Right: BR Standard 4MT no. 80142 was also in the Yard.

Bottom left: M7 0-4-4T no. 30053 was presenttogether with V class (Schools) 4-4-0 no. 30926 *Repton*. Both these engines were awaiting preservation overseas.

Top: Hampshire demu no. 1106 pulls into the Up Slow, Platform 2, at Eastleigh on 14th December 1963. The set still had the orange 'V' painted on before the change was made to the standard small yellow panel.

Bottom: BRCW (Birmingham Railway Carriage & Wagon) Type 3, now of course class 33, no. D6549 passes Eastleigh on the Down fast, 14th December 1963 with empty oil tanks for Fawley.

Right: Converted Battle of Britain no. 34058 *Sir Frederick Pile* is standing on the "New Road" of the Down side of Eastleigh station on 14th December 1963.

Keymer Junction.

Bottom: On 11th August 1963, 6PAN 3035 passes Keymer Junction with the 15.09 from Littlehampton to Victoria.

Right: 4LAV 2929 approaches Keymer Junction with the 13.47 from Victoria to Brighton also on 11th August 1963.

The prototype 4BEP unit no. 7001 has just passed Wivelsfield with a Down Brighton fast on 19th March 1967. The red cantrail colour indicates the restaurant / catering vehicle, with yellow for first-class..

This page: The primroses are out on the banks as all-blue 4CEP 7121 heads towards London on 16th April 1967. Common sense has prevailed with the red indicator blinds replacing the need for an oil tail lamp.
Opposite top: London Bridge to Brighton stopping service with 4LAV 2943 at Keymer Junction on 19th February 1966. Useful roof detail for the modeller is evident from the height of the overbridge.

Bottom: A certain amount of "pumping" is evident on the Up Fast at the crossover switch tips as unusually 4COR 3153 takes the 14.25 from Victoria to Eastbourne and Ore, 11th August 1963.

Above: The state of the Up Fast at Keymer Junction on 16th April 1967 certainly leaves something to be desired as 2HAL 2609 heads south with a Brighton stopping service. The author always thought that the provision of a black triangle on the front of a 2-car unit indicating the presence of the luggage compartment might have been improved – it would have made far more sense if the end WITHOUT the luggage compartment were shown! (after all, all 4-car sets had luggage compartments at both ends of the unit, and only railway enthusiasts would be able to tell the difference between a 2-car and a 4-car as it approached).

Opposite: 6PUL 3011 slows for the 20 mph turnout restriction to the Eastbourne line at Keymer Junction on 15th September 1963.

Bottom: The Up signal gantry from Epsom Downs at the London end of Sutton station, 30ᵗʰ May 1966. Why the station name has been painted out is subject to conjecture, after all, WW2 had finished more than twenty years before!

Right: The Up starting signals at Sutton for the Epsom line is to an unusual design – but dictated by the need for sighting on the approach - with the High Street and station overbridge in the way.

Brighton and the Belle.
Above: In its original livery of green/grey, E 6003 waits in Platform 7 at Brighton on 29th August 1967.

Top right: Battle of Britain class no. 34057 *Biggin Hill* stands in Platform 2 at Brighton ready to depart with the through service to Plymouth, 6th May 1961.

Bottom right: Known affectionately as "the Yellow Peril", A1X class Brighton Works shunter no. 32635 moves around the works on 6th May 1961. Originally no. 35 *Morden*, it was renumbered into Southern Railway Service stock as 377S in 1946, before in BR days renamed *Brighton Works* and given the number shown.

A ten-car train with unit 5BEL 3052 leading approaches Keymer Junction with the down Brighton Belle on 19th February 1966 – Wivelsfield station may be picked out just behind the train.

Right: 5BEL 3051 is in charge of the ten-car Brighton Belle on 7th March 1964 as it passes Burgess Hill. In 1968, we moved to a new house only some 300 yards away from this position – my elder son who was coming up to 3, was soon able to say "Brighton Belle, Mummy" as he heard the approach of the then unique motors fitted to the 5BEL units!

Bottom: Another view of the Down Brighton Belle, headed by 5BEL 3053, passing through Wivelsfield and with only 5 cars on this service. By this time, 15th April 1967, the Pullman coat of arms on the front has been replaced with the small yellow warning panel.

Left: 5BEL 3051 awaiting departure from Platform 5 in Brighton station on 31st July 1964.

Bottom left: 5BEL 3052 is under the future doomed arched roof of London Bridge, 15th November 1969. Due to the reconstruction of Grosvenor Bridge outside Victoria, the Belle was diverted over a few weekends.

Bottom right: Surprisingly 4COR 3125 heads the Brighton Belle with the 12.45 up working on 17th July 1971. The 4COR was being used while one of the other 5BEL units was being refurbished. It is seen here just south of Franklands Bridge between Hassocks and Burgess Hill. Was there still a supplementary charge?

Opposite: A classic location – the northern portal of Clayton Tunnel – showing the Up Brighton Belle formed of 5BEL 3051 on 5th August 1963. In those days, neither my wife or I drove a car so we had cycled over to Clayton from Burgess Hill just to take this photograph.

Just a short time before the train's demise, 5BEL 3051 forms the 11.00 Victoria to Brighton working, approaching Wivelsfield on 11th March 1972.

Saturday 6th April 1968.		Unit Nos. 3052 + 3051 (10 coaches)				
The Brighton Belle						
Station		**M.Ch.**	**d**	**Due**	**Actual**	**Speed**
Victoria		00-00	d	11.00	00 00	Time
Grosvenor Bridge, N end		00-57			01 45	19½
Battersea Park		01-24			02 54	45½/50
Pouparts Junction		02-00			03 44	49
Clapham Junction		02-58			04 39	54½
Wandsworth Common		04-06			06 07	57
Balham		04-51	p	11.07½	06 43	53½
Streatham Common		06-48			08 48	65
Norbury		07-34			09 35	62
Thornton Heath		08-54			10 58	46 sigs
Selhurst		09-31			11 54	52½
Windmill Bridge Junction		9-77/60	p	11.13	12 43	26 sigs
East Croydon		10-29			13 50	37
South Croydon		11-24			15 01	51
Purley Oaks		12-35			16 16	59
Purley		13-29			17 14	60
Coulsdon North		14-67	p	11.19	18 45	45½*
Star Lane Signalbox		16-63			21 07	53½
Quarry Tunnel, N Portal		17-24			21 41	50
Quarry Tunnel, S Portal		18-40			22 52	67½
Redhill Tunnel, N Portal		20-62			24 44	77 max
Redhill Tunnel, S Portal		21-11			25 05	62
Earlswood		21-50	p	11.26	25 38	62
Salfords		23-35			27 11	77
Horley		25-60			28 53	83½
Gatwick Airport		26-45			29 32	81
Tinsley Green	U	27-36			30 12	79
Three Bridges		29-22	p	11.33½	31 39	76
Balcombe Tunnel Signalbox		31-53	p	11.36	33 38	71 min
Balcombe Tunnel, S Portal		32-54			34 29	75
Balcombe		33-67			35 24	80
Ouse Valley Viaduct, N end		35-37			36 35	84
Copyhold Junction	D	36-42			37 20	87
Haywards Heath		37-58			38 09	87
Haywards Heath Tunnel, SP		38-16			38 30	89
Folly Farm	U	39-44			39 24	90
Wivelsfield		40-50			40 09	89
Keymer Junction		40-69	p	11.44	40 20	87
Burgess Hill		41-34			40 43	83½
Hassocks		43-43			42 17	78½
Clayton Tunnel, N Portal		44-44			43 05	74
Clayton Tunnel, S Portal		45-66			44 10	70½
Clayton Cutting Signalbox	U	46-14			44 27	71½/77
Patcham Tunnel, N Portal		47-65			45 46	68
Patcham Tunnel, S Portal		48-07			46 01	Brakes
Preston Park		49-20			47 26	41/25 sigs
Upper Goods Signalbox	D	49-72			48 45	33
Brighton		50-50	a	11.55	50 20	-

By 1968, the timing for the Brighton Belle had been reduced to 55 minutes for the 50¾ miles, and with the heavy amount of traffic particularly on the two track section south of Balcombe Junction, this was not easy to maintain. Of the sixteen runs of the Belle that your author has timed over the years, the one shown [below] must be judged the best. The 5 BEL units were introduced with the electrification of the Brighton line, entering service on 1st January 1933. They were given 60 minutes for the journey, and were limited to 75 mph. 4CIG units were allowed to run up to 90 mph when the line speed was raised to 90 mph in 1967, but not the HALs, BILs, LAVs, CORs, PULs, and BELs! Hence the maximum speed quoted in the example shown at 90 mph was not actually exceeding the line speed, but it was slightly over the top for a 35-year old!

Wivelsfield.
The only 4CIG unit to have a wrap-round yellow end was no. 7303, seen here in Wivelsfield Up platform with the gas lamp still illuminated - even though this was just before lunchtime on 2nd September 1967.

Next page top: 4LAV 2926 runs into Wivelsfield with a Brighton stopping train, 2nd September 1967.

Next page bottom: Hassocks, with 4LAV 2952 on an 8-car stopping service to Brighton, 11th April 1964. The down platform awning behind the train was blown down in a severe gale only a few weeks later.

Top left: An unusual working on the Brighton line saw 4SUB 4647 on a stopping at Wivelsfield on 15th April 1967. The oil lamp will be noted.

Top right: At Wivelsfield on 2nd September 1967, the Up and Down Eastbourne trains pass each other – the Up train is headed by 4CIG 7315 and will run via the Quarry Line to Victoria. The 4CIGs had replaced the 6PUL/6PANs during the previous year, while the 4VEPs replaced the 4LAVs on semi-fast workings during this year.

Bottom: The old order. On 5th March 1966, 4LAV 2930 approaches Gatwick Airport, now being extended on the eastern side.

Before the site was totally reconstructed for the passage of HS1, BRCW Type 3 no. D6519 approaches the old Platform 3 at Ashford. The date is 4th August 1962. The stock is formed of at least one Maunsell design set.

DEMU 6-car unit no. 1032 stands in Platform 3 at Hastings. The bland appearance to the front end of these trains was similar to that used soon after for the Hampshire DEMU sets.

Right: The RCTS ran a farewell to the Brighton Belle on 8th April 1972, but took it to Eastbourne! The working is seen here crossing Ditchling Common, a mile or so east of Keymer Junction.

Bottom: Saturday 19th March 1967 was billed as the "Last Day of Steam on the Brighton line" – West Country no. 34108 *Wincanton* heads the last steam train, although not quite on the Brighton line, instead crossing Ditchling Common a mile or so before the Brighton main line.

To and on the Isle of Wight
Left: 4COR 3123 leads an Up Portsmouth Harbour fast, just east of Surbiton on 4th June 1965.

Opposite top left: Near Lake, W31 *Chale* heads south on 28th June 1966.

Opposite top right: W35 *Freshwater* approaches Ryde St Johns from Smallbrook Junction, 3rd September 1965 with a train for Ryde Pier Head.

Right: The old Southern Railway paddle steamer *Ryde* heads away across the Spithead to Portsmouth on 4th September 1965.

Opposite bottom: Running bunker first back to Ryde on 30th June 1966, is W17 *Seaview*.

W16 *Ventnor* seen heading south near Lake, 30th June 1966.

Above: Coach no. S4165 standing in the platform at Ventnor on 3rd September 1965.

Above: W26 *Whitwell* is about to depart north from Ventnor into the single track tunnel immediately off the platform end on 3rd September 1965 under St Boniface Down.
Bottom right: Seen running round its coaches at the Ventnor terminus is no. W20 *Shanklin,* 24th November 1961.
These 0-4-4T class 02 tanks were classified as only 'OP'.

W24 *Calbourne* meets W18 *Ningwood* at Wroxall, 3rd September 1965. *Calbourne* is the only survivor of the O2 class and still exists on the preservation line at Haven Street.

The Windsor side of Waterloo station complete with its magnificent roof and six trains occupying the 6 platforms. The date is 1st April 1972. All this has since been demolished and replaced with what are now the now redundant Eurostar platforms. Left to right the set types are 2EPBs numbered 56XX, then 4CIG 7420, 4CIG 7396, 4SUB 4289 and finally 4SUB 4717. This was also a time when the railway still carried mail!

Special working

Above: The LCGB special of 19th March 1966, seen here at Southampton Terminus with two USA tanks in charge, 30073 + 30064.

Right: The special at Fawley and with no 30073 in the process of running round.

The special involved no 33006 from Eastleigh to Gosport and thence to Southampton Terminus. Here the two tank engines took over for the run to Fawley and return to Totton. No 33006 then took over again to Lymington Pier and back to Brockenhurst, Unusually this was a tour which did not start and end at the same station.